Aayush Upadhyay

Behind the Ivy Curtain

Analyzing nearly 5,000 Admission Results

for a Data Driven Guide to Elite College Admissions

Dedication

To my high school principal Mr. Bernie Montero. Words can't do justice, but thanks for everything you did for me and continue to do for others.

Table Of Contents

About the Author

I grew up in Miramar, Florida and attended Somerset Academy Charter High School. I am a recent graduate of Yale with a Bachelors and Masters in Computer Science. Right now I work at Google and live in San Francisco, California. I enjoy all forms of sports and like running, biking, playing basketball, and trash talking.

I have been tutoring students all throughout high school and college, and have spent far too many hours over the years scouring the web for admissions advice. Luckily it's all packaged here for you to soak up.

Introduction

What Is This Book About?

This is a high-level guide to college admissions. I talk about what happens after you send in your college application and how it's evaluated by admission officers, and what you'll need to do to maximize your odds of admission.

Going a little deeper, it's about *elite* college admissions. I discuss the eight Ivy League Schools (Brown, Columbia, Cornell, Dartmouth, Harvard, University of Pennsylvania, Princeton, and Yale) and Stanford and MIT for a total of ten schools. This group is sometimes referred to as the Ivy Plus, but the grouping is arbitrary.

There are lots of other great and elite schools like the University of Chicago or Duke, and the concepts discussed in this book apply to them too. For better or worse, the US News & World Report makes an annual ranking of undergraduate colleges and universities. Our advice applies to most of the top-ranked schools (say the top 50 or so).

Going a little deeper, you'll see that the subtitle is "*A Data Driven Guide to Elite College Admissions.*" The "data driven" part differentiates this book from everything else out there. I collected information from admission results **for nearly 5,000 students** spanning the **classes of 2013-2018** and analyzed it to find patterns, or a lack of patterns, and concretely establish what works and what doesn't in terms of getting into elite colleges.

So other people can give general advice like "you need a high SAT" or "start a club," but I looked at the concrete data to get a level of granularity like never before. This means we can answer questions like "I got a 2290 on my SAT and I want to go to Harvard. Is it worth it to retake?" and you can read outcomes from the last five years to figure out what to do (Spoiler: the numbers say don't retake.)

So overall, this book analyzes historical admissions data and combines it with a knowledge of how the admissions process works to help you maximize your odds of elite college admission success.

Who Is This For?

I hope this book is fun and interesting for students, parents, counselors, teachers, or just people curious about peeking behind the Ivy League curtain. There are many myths out there about what kinds of prodigies get into elite schools, and I hope that the data driven nature of this book can shed some light into what kinds of people get in.

That being said, a large part of this book is about how to actually improve your own college application based on the information. Thus, the main audience is students in high school or entering high school. The perfect readers would be students entering 9th or 10th grade. Students at that level have the most time to do meaningful things and set themselves up for admissions success. Even if you're already in 10th or 11th grade, you'll read plenty of interesting information. You can understand what to focus on to maximize your admissions odds. As a side note, I did not seriously think about going to a top school until sophomore spring of high school, and I was admitted to various Ivy League and other top schools and eventually went to Yale.

People often tell you "it's never too late to make a plan," but let us be clear: if you start looking at top schools senior year of high school, it is too late. Don't know the difference between Brown and Dartmouth? Sure, you can fix that pretty quickly. Never did any extracurriculars until summer of your junior year? That's probably a nail in the coffin for most applications. The sooner you start, the better off you are.

A Note To Parents

I hope that many parents of high school students read this book. I was very lucky to have two parents who were very supportive through my high school years. As a result, I don't think I was ever really stressed in high school—definitely not because of academics. On the flip side, I met many kids in my freshman year at Yale who were burned out from their high schools; there was too much work in school and their parents were too overbearing.

Many parents think you need perfect scores, flawless grades, ability to play an instrument, and a couple other "resume building" things to get into a top school. The implication is that if you don't get into a top school, both the parent and the student have failed. This logic is wrong for so many reasons, but two of the biggest ones are:
1. Most common elite college admission advice is wrong. You don't need perfect grades, and you don't need to play violin and tennis or volunteer 200 hours. There are many ways to get in, but imitating what's worked for others actually handicaps you.
2. Not getting into an elite college is not the end of the world. There are many great institutions in the United States. Ultimately, if you raise a child who is independent and driven, he or she will succeed no matter where they go.

"I want to succeed academically" is a good strategy for anyone, but "I have to get into MIT" is not a strategy, it's a wish. Much of the admission process is outside your hands, and you should be working to encourage your child instead of adding needless pressure.

Data Sources

All the data behind this book was gathered from the College Confidential Forums at http://talk.collegeconfidential.com. Every year, many students self report their admission profile and outcomes. There is always some variability in the fields entered, but roughly the template is:

Objective:

SAT I (breakdown):
ACT:
SAT II:
Unweighted GPA (out of 4.0):
Rank (percentile if rank is unavailable):
AP (place score in parenthesis):
IB (place score in parenthesis):
Senior Year Course Load:
Major Awards (USAMO, Intel etc.):

Subjective:

Extracurriculars (place leadership in parenthesis):
Job/Work Experience:
Volunteer/Community service:
Summer Activities:
Essays:
Teacher Recommendation:
Counselor Rec:
Additional Rec:
Interview:

Other:

State (if domestic applicant):
Country (if international applicant):
School Type:
Ethnicity:
Gender:
Income Bracket:
Hooks (URM, first generation college, etc.):

Reflection:

Strengths:
Weaknesses:
Why you think you were accepted/waitlisted/rejected:
Where else were you accepted/waitlisted/rejected:

Each school has a sub-forum on the website where kids regularly post and wait for results to come out. All the data was collected from various "results" threads from 2013-2018, both for early action and regular decision. The information is self-reported so it's not 100% trustworthy, but as a member of the community and former poster I know that almost all of it is legitimate. These kids have spent months, if not years, going through the process together and there's a strong urge to give back to the community.

I wrote a scraper and parser to collect all the info and convert it into a nice format for analyzing and getting rid of bad results. All in all, there were 4,888 admission results with useable data. If you want access to my scrapers and scripts, please email me at topcollegeadmit@gmail.com and I'm happy to provide the raw sources.

How Can You Utilize This Info?

The book uses this information to identify the impact of various parts of the application and come up with thresholds and recommendations—actionable things you can do to boost your chances of admission.

Much of our analysis is about the numerical factors (scores, rank, GPA) because these factors are easier to process, average, and use to make claims. For the subjective info, we analyzed sentiment and combined that with what we know about the admissions process to draw conclusions.

You are welcome to go through the raw data if you're curious about what was actually on some of these profiles. For the biggest bang for your buck though, I'd recommend you just read the book through or skip to the Conclusions section to get the takeaways. It's easy to suffer from "analysis paralysis" so I tried to be very concrete about what we're looking at and its impact on admissions.

Why Did I Write This Book?

To be honest, I've been thinking about writing this book since 2008.

For me, high school was one of those "big fish, small pond" scenarios—I had some really cool teachers and great friends, but I was rarely challenged academically and spent most of my time being a smart-aleck. I never tried too hard until sophomore spring where I decided that I wanted to leave South Florida and go out of state. I realized that the best way to do that was to get into a top college. I spent hundreds of hours over the next two years reading about how to prepare for exams and about how other kids have done it before me.

I had a pretty relaxed time in high school but in April and May, I'd crank things up to do well on AP exams and I put in the work to do well on the SAT and Subject Tests. I also started some clubs in school and tutored in a variety of subjects. In addition, I gave presentations on test prep and college admission in my high school and helped kids apply to Ivies even after I graduated. Basically, I learned a ton of information and wanted to share as much as I could.

People charge tons of money for this info—it is ridiculous that some pay thousands of dollars for info that's freely available. Your guidance counselor is overwhelmed by students and often time can't even give you the right advice. My counselor was an awesome lady but her first year as a counselor was my senior year and I was the first kid in my school's short history aiming for an Ivy League university, so she had no experience or advice to give me there.

So that's the motivation for me. There's so much great advice online, and I wanted to consolidate it all and back it up with data for kids like "high school Aayush"—smart and motivated, but big fishes in small ponds. This book is the end result.

Without further adieu, let's get started!

Behind the Admissions Process

What Is This Section About?

This part of the book goes into how the admissions process works. We start with how and when you apply, then talk about what happens when you submit your application. This is the real "behind the scenes" part. It was collated from information out on the web and discussions with people who have worked in admission offices at these top schools.

You can skip this if you want and go straight to the admission factors section, which has the data analysis, but this section is really crucial for setting the environment.

Life Of An Application

The admissions process begins senior year of high school. Students visit colleges or attend talks from admission officers as they do regional tours. Schools pass out pamphlets with information on universities, financial aid, etc. Some of you will probably just look at the US News top 25 schools and apply to all of them. This is a dumb idea but I won't stop you. College fit is very important and the best way to figure that out is to visit the school. If you can't, read everything you can online and talk to students to get an idea of the campus environment. I'm going to assume that you'll do the research here and figure out where you want to apply.

Common Application

So now you've got your list of schools. As of 2015, most schools will accept the Common Application (www.commonapp.org), where you enter your details (demographic, extracurricular, academic), submit your recommenders, and write an essay that every school can see.

We won't go through the Common App in detail here, but it's worth exploring the components. The demographic part is long but straightforward: name, residence, info about parents, high school, etc. The academic part involves your GPA/rank, test scores, senior year course load, and awards/honors you've received. The extracurricular activities section asks you to categorize your main activities and list how involved you were and what you achieved. Finally there's a 250-500 word essay on one of the following topics:

1. *Evaluate a significant experience, achievement, risk you have taken, or ethical dilemma you have faced and its impact on you.*
2. *Discuss some issue of personal, local, national, or international concern and its importance to you.*
3. *Indicate a person who has had a significant influence on you, and describe that influence.*
4. *Describe a character in fiction, a historical figure, or a creative work (as in art, music, science, etc.) that has had an influence on you, and explain that influence.*
5. *A range of academic interests, personal perspectives, and life experiences adds much to the educational mix. Given your personal background, describe an experience that illustrates what you would bring to the diversity in a college community or an encounter that demonstrated the importance of diversity to you.*
6. *Topic of your choice.*

Many schools also require a Common App supplement, usually an essay and/or a few short questions. The University of Chicago is famous for cool essay questions. You can get the full list at https://collegeadmissions.uchicago.edu/apply/essay-questions, but here's my favorite of this year:

"Little pigs, french hens, a family of bears. Blind mice, musketeers, the Fates. Parts of an atom, laws of thought, a guideline for composition. Omne trium perfectum? Create your own group of threes, and describe why and how they fit together."

And that wraps up what you have to do for the Common Application. The rest involves nominating your counselor and two teachers for recommendations. They create an account and upload their "recs" separately. Once it's all in, you pick the schools you want to apply to, pay the application fees, and click submit!

App In Transit

Once you submit your application, it lands in the school's admissions office through a series of intermediate software. A PDF is generated, and the data is stored in some servers provided by a company like Technolutions (https://technolutions.com/). The details are irrelevant. After a series of hoops, it lands in the admissions office and is eventually reviewed by admissions officers.

Admission Office Review

(Note: I have not personally worked in an admissions office, but the content in this section was collated from interviews with people who have. The FERPA act also lets you see your admissions profile once you're admitted, so much of the info was cross examined there.)

This is the really interesting part. When an application comes in, it is assigned to an admissions officer based on your region. The admissions officer spends about 20-25 minutes going through your application and trying to build an image of who you are. There is an entire code language they use. A phrase like "top ac" means top academic credentials—all your scores and grades condensed into one comment! There's commentary on how the essays, recommendations, and activities come together to represent you. They are trying to get a sense of *who you are as a person*.

There's a common statement made that 70% of the applicants to a top school are academically qualified to get in. Kinda shocking isn't it? Many of you will be the top students in your schools and nobody else is even close, so can you imagine tens of thousands of kids as smart and hard working as you trying to get in? That's what the admissions office deals with. That's why the written part of the application is so important. Your grades won't differentiate you after a certain point, so it's the character elements—your "story" so to speak—which controls your admissions destiny.

Finally, there's a section to give an overall rating and ratings for your academics, extracurriculars, counselor recommendation, teacher recommendation, and interview. The overall rating scale varies from school to school, but it's usually from 1-4 with +/-'s. Getting a "1" means you are in the top 5-10% of candidates and really excellent. A "4" means you're basically out. Most others fall in the 2-3 range. A "2+" is promising, and getting in the "3" range is not a dealbreaker but it will be much tougher to get in. For the specific areas (academics, extracurriculars, etc), a score is given from 1-9, where 5 is middle of the pack. 8's and 9's are rare here, and getting a few 6's/7's will help you.

Anyways, after the first reader finishes reading your application and writing comments, the application is passed on to a second reader who is either another admissions officer, a professor, or someone outside the college who is trusted to read applications. They also evaluate you, and then you're off to the "adcom" or admissions committee.

Admissions Committee (Adcom)

The adcom is a group of people, mainly admissions officers and the Dean of admissions but sometimes professors or external people, who go through your application and make an "Accept/Reject/Waitlisted" decision. The adcom convenes in the last couple weeks before results are released and they work non-stop to evaluate everyone.

The evaluation process is simple. Everyone has a paper copy of your reviews and your admissions officer makes a case for why they should admit you. There is usually a spirited discussion about your achievements and character and how you'll fit into the campus environment. Your application is usually grouped with people from your region since your admissions officer is trying to make a case for all of his or her applicants. At the end the committee makes a decision and they move on.

And that wraps up the life of an application. The process is the same for early admission/decision, except most schools defer more liberally than they do in regular decision. At the end, either you get in or you don't; there's no appeal process. For some of you, waitlisting is an outcome. The odds are awful—at a top school, hundreds of students are waitlisted and only about 10-20 come off the waitlist.

Academic Index

The Academic Index (AI) is a number ranging from 60-240 that summarizes your academic performance based on Class Rank & Size, SAT I (or scaled ACT), and SAT II scores. This AI number is scaled differently at different schools, but the basic idea is that higher AI = stronger candidate academically. Michelle Hernandez was the first person to publicly talk about AI in her book "A is for Admissions." It's very interesting and goes into more detail about some of the information covered in this section. I'd recommend it if you're eager to learn more.

This number was originally used for Ivy League athletic recruiting. Teams have to have AI's in certain bands close to the school's median AI. Ivy League schools have a median AI of 210-220, though obviously they don't publish this. Different schools scale it differently, but having an AI greater than 225 should put you in a great position academically.

The higher your AI, the stronger you are academically. The AI is computed by scaling your SAT/ACT, SAT2 scores, and your class rank/percentile. Here is the formula:

SAT = ((Reading score + Writing score)/2 + Math score)/20
SAT2 = (Highest SAT2 + 2nd Highest SAT2)/20
Rank = Based on a scale, either using GPA or percentile.

Source: New York Times
Links to Rank scales

Various Academic Index Calculators exist, and you can find two at:
College Confidential
satscores.us

Some schools have now removed the SAT Subject Test requirements, so it's unclear as to how they'll adjust the Academic Index. As for the calculators, some use GPA, others use class rank, and they all use slightly different formulas but are all pretty close. These scores are scaled to a single digit number, sometimes from 1-5 or 1-9. According to satscore.us, the scaling is as follows:

AI	AI Rank	Chance at Ivy League
>230	9	Excellent
225-229	8	Very Good
221-224	7	Good
216-220	6	Above Average

211-215	5	Average
203-210	4	Below Average
193-202	3	Low
181-192	2	Very Low
<180	1	Almost impossible

Be cautious with treating this as a certainty though. To quote from a New York Times article on the topic:

"'When a teacher says on a recommendation, 'This person is the brightest student I've ever taught,' that jumps off the page,' Mr. Goldberger said. 'Or if the teacher writes that a particular student was more inventive at problem-solving than any student in the school for the last four years, that kind of thing sky-rockets an applicant beyond any number.

'There is always the human element. Some things don't translate into numbers.'"

Source: New York Times

Special Situations/Hooks (Recruits, Legacies, URM)

A hook refers to some unique characteristic that gives you an admission edge. The first kid who built a shelter in South America could've used that story as his hook; now many more kids do it so it's not differentiating.

A hook can be an international level award like an International Mathematics Olympiad (IMO) medal, starring in major movies like Emma Watson, competing in the Olympics, etc. Generally, a hook is something that makes you clearly exceptional, and if you're reading this book then you probably don't have a hook. There are a few special situations that we'll go through here:

Athletic Recruiting

If you're a recruited athlete, you are in. Schools have different allocations for different sports, and there are Ivy League guidelines for recruiting. The big thing is that your academics can be worse than the median, but they still has to be within a range. I'm no expert here and there's plenty of material online, but if you're good enough to be all-state or winning tournaments and have a 2000+ SAT, look into being recruited.

Legacies

If you had a parent or relative attend an Ivy League school, you have a much higher chance of getting in. At Princeton legacies have a 30-40% acceptance rate depending on which source you pick. From a Business Insider article about Princeton President Christopher Eisgruber[1]:

Asked whether it was fair that nearly 30 percent of legacies were admitted last year while the overall admission rate was 7.4 percent, Eisgruber said the higher admission rate for legacies was "about right."

"It's a recognition of a special bond that Princeton has with its alumni and it matters so much to the University," Eisgruber said. "That preference is literally a tie-breaker in cases where credentials are about even."

Nobody tries to hide it and almost every top school has a preference for legacies. If you are one, milk it for what it's worth.

---

[1] http://www.businessinsider.com/princeton-university-president-legacy-applicants-2013-10

Underrepresented Minority (URM)

If you're Black, Hispanic, or Native American, you will get an admissions boost. Much has been discussed about affirmative action and it's too nuanced to discuss here. Some argue it's a slight boost and others say it's significant. I don't think there's enough concrete public numbers to end the debate. You can Google around for "ivy league affirmative action" to see what people have said.

This is something you don't control though. Focus on building the most compelling application and let the chips fall where they may.

Geography

This is kind of a stretch hook, i.e. usually irrelevant. If you're from an underrepresented state like Arkansas, then it may be a little easier for you to get in. We will go through the numbers later in the book but there's not much of a hook here.

Conclusion

In this section of the book we walked through the admissions process, explaining what goes into your application and how it's evaluated. We've discussed the specific metrics and also gone through hooks and special situations that give your application a boost.

Espenshade, Chung, and Walling published a paper in 2004 called "Admission Preferences for Minority Students, Athletes, and Legacies at Elite Universities"[2]:

TABLE 1

Sample Characteristics and Percent of Applicants Admitted

Category	Number of Applicants	Percent of Applicants	Percent Admitted
Total Sample	124,374	100.0	25.0
Cohort			
1980s[a]	40,825	32.8	24.5
1993	38,000	30.6	29.1
1997	45,549	36.6	21.9
Sex			
Male	68,465	55.0	24.1
Female	55,909	45.0	25.9
Citizenship			
U.S.	105,959	85.2	26.4
Non-U.S.	18,415	14.8	16.5
SAT Score			
< 1000	2,643	2.1	1.9
1000–1099	4,967	4.0	5.8
1100–1199	12,180	9.8	12.2
1200–1299	23,287	18.7	17.5
1300–1399	32,603	26.2	24.0
1400–1499	29,486	23.7	33.2
1500–1600	14,440	11.6	48.7
Unknown	4,768	3.8	10.2
Race			
White	60,620	48.7	26.9
African American	6,618	5.3	38.7
Hispanic	6,906	5.6	31.6
Asian	28,754	23.1	20.9
Other[b]	21,476	17.3	18.6
Athlete			
No	116,897	94.0	23.4
Yes	7,477	6.0	49.1
Legacy			
No	119,649	96.2	24.0
Yes	4,725	3.8	49.7

[a]The 1980s entering classes represented by the three institutions in our analysis correspond to the fall of 1982, 1985, and 1986.

[b]"Other" race includes race not specified.

Source: National Study of College Experience.

The numbers speak for themselves. Athletes, Legacies, and URMs all have a higher admission rate than their counterparts. The numbers here are obviously old and the next section of this

---

[2]

http://www.princeton.edu/~tje/files/files/webAdmission%20Preferences%20Espenshade%20Chung%20Walling%20Dec%202004.pdf book looks at current numbers from what we've gathered, but there's a strong indication that hooks live up to the hype.

Behind Individual Factors

What Is This Section About?

In this section we'll go through the data analysis. We will go through all the major "metrics" from the previous section and look at actual admission results and make some interesting conclusions.

Again, this data was collected from scraping admission result posts from College Confidential (CC). We gathered data for nearly 5,000 students over a six-year period (2009-2014), corresponding to the college classes of 2013-2018, and parsed and extracted as much as we could. You can email me at topcollegeadmit@gmail.com to download the data with instructions on how to play around with it yourself.

Please note that the CC forums have a bias towards kids who are reading about college admissions and actively trying to optimize their profiles. They're not representative of the total candidate pool—there is certainly a bias towards the top end academically. Still, if you're reading this book, then you're probably similar to the average CC'er, and even if you're not, there are many conclusions we can draw even from this data.

The focus of this section is to examine each factor in isolation. That way we can see if any single factor gives you a major boost.

And with that, let's begin!

Academic Factors

SAT

One of the most common questions is "What SAT score do I need to get into a top school?"

Outcome	Average SAT	Students
Accepted	2257.16	1446
Deferred/Waitlisted	2252.19	789
Rejected	2239.53	663

Over 3,000 students posted SAT scores, and the differences are negligible. One question separates the average rejected SAT from the average accepted SAT. Let's stratify this by score bands to see if the outcome changes based on how high you scored:

SAT Range	Accepted	Deferred/Waitlisted	Rejected	Total	% Accepted
2400	94	42	31	167	56.29
2300-2399	592	319	241	1152	51.39
2200-2299	429	223	194	846	50.71
2100-2199	180	107	111	398	45.23
2000-2099	89	64	56	209	42.59
< 2000	62	34	30	126	49.21
Total	1446	789	663	2898	49.90

So a perfect score isn't a guarantee for admission. What's interesting to me is that all the "% Accepted" values are basically the same. We can't use normal statistical tools since this isn't a random sample, and the fact that half the reporters were accepted is way higher than the normal 10-15% overall admit rate you'd expect.

It's interesting that the acceptance rate is so high for the < 2000. I dug into this and the numbers are deceptive. Some kids scored in the 30's in the ACT and were more competitive in that band, so the SAT isn't representative. Other kids were clearly hooked (URMs, recruits, etc.), the most extreme example being:

Decision: Accepted (Wharton)
SAT I (breakdown): 1780 (580M 610R 590W)
Rank (percentile if rank is unavailable): 30% percentile

Additional Rec: Had a recommendation from Sen. John McCain
Income Bracket: ~$5M+
Hooks (URM, first generation college, etc.): legacy (I will be 4th generation, my great grandfather, grandfather, and father all went to Penn), significant family donations

If a former presidential candidate is writing you a recommendation and you're a fourth generation legacy, your SAT score won't be the deciding factor ;)

Anyways, the 2000's have the lowest admit rate and that seems to reflect the set of students who are "giving it a shot" but their scores just aren't competitive. The rest of the brackets are pretty much the same, which implies that having a 2100+ score should be sufficient. This translates to about 700 in each section of the SAT. The 2100 row has half the entries of the other rows though, so if you want to play it safe, aim for a 2200+. We can reasonably conclude that **a 2200+ score means you won't get rejected due to your score.**

A higher score doesn't guarantee admission, while a low score will disqualify you unless you're hooked. Finally, we have scores by schools in the appendix if you're interested, but the numbers don't vary significantly.

ACT

Outcome	Average ACT	Students
Accepted	33.42	597
Deferred/Waitlisted	33.47	356
Rejected	33.34	355

Even closer than the SAT bands. If you could only see the ACT score of an application, you would have terrible odds at guessing whether they got in or not, unless…

ACT Range	Accepted	Deferred/Waitlisted	Rejected	Total	% Accepted
36	68	33	34	135	50.37
34-35	288	173	172	633	45.50
33	78	54	48	180	43.33
32	58	47	34	139	41.73
30-31	72	34	45	151	47.68
< 30	33	15	22	70	47.14
Total	597	356	355	1308	45.64

Just kidding, there's no unless. The admit rates are a little lower than SAT rates, but the sample isn't big enough to make any sweeping conclusion. It appears that the ACT bands are similar to the SAT bands. The lowest scores probably indicate hooked applicants, and among the top range you are doing enough to be competitive but admit rates are similar across these bands. That indicates that the rest of the application is where the difference is.

Given the number of reports, I'd say that a **33-34** is a great score to check off the "test score" box. Don't worry about re-testing after that. The numbers suggest 30-31 is high enough, but I don't think there are enough entries to be confident. The takeaway is that scoring in this range should be enough to check the test checkbox.

GPA

"Is my GPA high enough?" is another common question that students ask. Here we're talking about unweighted GPA, i.e. out of a 4.0 scale where an A = 4, B = 3, C = 2, etc. Naturally you want to take a tough course load, but we'll go into the specifics of "tough" in a later section. Here are the stats by GPA:

GPA Range	Accepted	Deferred/Waitlisted	Rejected	Total	% Accepted
4	651	358	240	1249	52.12
3.9-3.99	451	257	245	953	47.32
3.8-3.89	148	100	93	341	43.40
3.7-3.79	67	47	60	174	38.51
3.6-3.69	19	15	20	54	35.19
3.5-3.59	10	4	6	20	50
3.0-3.4	12	6	15	33	36.36
< 3.0	2	0	0	2	100
Total	1360	787	679	2826	48.12

There is a clear positive association between GPA and acceptance rate, ignoring the small samples at the bottom. **The higher your GPA, the better you'll do.** You can't just "retest" a GPA so the obvious conclusion is to get grades as high as you can.

There is an interesting question though: should you take tougher courses and hurt your GPA or take easier courses and have a higher GPA? It's difficult to answer this because we don't have transcript histories in the data scraped, but the admission committee looks at your grades and what courses you got them in. So the decision is contingent on a few things:

- Will taking an extra AP class hurt your GPA? What do you project your grades for that semester to be?
- Will this class move you up a tier in the "schedule difficulty" rating in the counselor recommendation?
- Are you interested in the material or are you just doing it for college? To be honest this should be the only question, but a combination of environmental factors and competitive goals will make you ignore this and focus on the previous questions. I'm not going to judge, but you should acknowledge the fact.

In general, challenge yourself, but only enough to get the "most challenging" recommendation. You're not going to benefit "admissions wise" from taking more courses unless you tie it to the rest of your application to show some specific interest. Taking a bunch of AP classes is not going to blow anyone away.

Rank (Percentile)

What impact does rank have on admit rates? Some kids give an absolute rank like 1st or 2nd or 3rd, while others give percentiles. Since they also generally give class size, we converted everything into percentiles. Without further adieu, here is the data:

Rank (Percentile)	Accepted	Deferred/Waitlisted	Rejected	Total	% Accepted
1	553	308	250	1111	49.77
2 - 5	176	104	99	379	46.44
6 - 10	135	86	82	303	44.55
11 - 20	31	21	28	80	38.75
21 - 30	6	6	3	15	40
30 - 100	4	1	1	6	66.67
Total	905	526	463	1894	47.78

This one is pretty correlated with unweighted GPA and we see the same trend here—the higher your rank, the higher your acceptance rate. NO reason not to strive to go as high as you can.

There is a discussion about how important it is to be #1 versus being in the top 1% or top 5% or something like that. We know that 49.77% is the acceptance rate for being in the top 1%. If you look at the top 2%, the rate is 50.04%, and the rate for the top 3% is 49.01%. So basically the numbers are the same. Try to get as high a rank as you can, but don't stress about being valedictorian or salutatorian.

Course Load

Students often ask which courses to take, whether to go AP or not, and the impact of it all. You can answer some of those questions without doing anything special. Every guidance counselor fills out a Common App Secondary School Report (CASSR). You can Google around to find a copy and we found one here. There are some questions on your GPA and how the school ranks and weighs GPA, and there are questions about the highest GPA in the class. Your course load obviously plays a role here, but there's an entire section just on what your school's courses look like. Here are the questions:

- How many courses does your school offer:
    - List number of AP
    - List number of IB
    - List number of Honors
- If school policy limits the number a student may take in a given year, please list the maximum allowed:
    - List number of AP
    - List number of IB
    - List number of Honors
- Is the applicant an IB Diploma candidate? (Yes/No)
- Are classes taken on a block schedule? (Yes/No)
- In comparison with other college preparatory students at your school, the applicant's course selection is:
    - most demanding
    - very demanding
    - demanding
    - average
    - below average

The first couple of questions give context to the adcom for what's possible at your school. Let's say you take 8 AP courses by the time you apply. If there are 25 AP courses offered but nobody can take more than 10, then you're in great shape. If there's no such limit and other candidates have taken 14-15 AP courses, then you look relatively weaker.

That's why the last question is a big one. You want to optimize for a schedule that gets you the "most demanding" rating. Don't bother with what the Internet says or what your friends at other schools are doing; talk to your counselor and figure out what qualifies as "most demanding" and do that. You can obviously do more, and do things like dual enrollment at a local college, but make sure you hit the threshold for most demanding.

That's why the data on course load is not very useful to people because it's all relative to your school. On the forums, students post what their senior year course load is to give you an idea of the degree of difficulty of their schedule. We parsed the data to see how many AP/IB courses the student was taking, and here's the data on # of tough courses senior year vs. admissions outcome:

# of AP/IB Courses	Accepted	Deferred/Waitlisted	Rejected	Total	% Accepted
1	349	201	161	711	49.09
2 - 3	332	319	229	880	37.73
4 - 5	541	319	229	1089	49.68
6 - 8	222	141	125	488	45.49
9+	8	10	2	20	40
Total	1452	990	746	3188	45.55

Good sample sizes here, but nothing big to take away. All the numbers are pretty close and it's hard to generalize this across a population because of the specifics of schools. So don't put much faith in these numbers—ask older students and your guidance counselor, figure out what makes a competitive schedule, and go get it!

AP Scores

Another common question is how AP scores impact admissions. The prevalent wisdom is that they are just meant as a check against grade inflation—if you have a great GPA but are failing your AP exams, then something is up. Otherwise AP scores are just for placement in courses and not a big deal in admissions.

This is partly false because the applications that the adcom uses to evaluate you will have your AP scores listed there as part of your academic profile. You shouldn't totally ignore AP exam scores, but note that the data backs up their relevance as a "check":

Reported Any:	Accepted	Deferred/Waitlisted	Rejected	Average Number of Scores Reported	Total	% Accepted
1s or 2s	30	17	29	1.14	76	39.47
3s	197	104	121	1.24	422	46.68
4s	589	323	314	1.52	1226	48.04
5s	1067	506	448	2.82	2021	52.80

This table is a little confusing so let me walk through the columns:
- **Reported Any** - Did the student report any of the following scores? So in the "1s and 2s" row it means, did we have a student report any AP scores of 1 or 2.
- **Accepted/Deferred/Rejected** - Standard. What the outcome was for that student.
- **Average Number of Scores Reported** - If a student did report a score in that bucket, how many did they report on average. So students with 1s/2s reported a little over 1 score on average, while students with 5s tended to report 5's on almost three exams on average.
- **Total** - How many students represent this observation.
- **% Accepted** - The acceptance rate.

Given these stats, it appears that there's no big difference between getting 3s, 4s, or 5s, although it increases slightly. Getting 1s and 2s seems to have a decent drop, but nothing that would be a clear dealbreaker. So the conclusion would be that you want to aim for 5s, but don't sweat it if you get 3s or 4s.

A related question is about the number of 5's that you get. Does it matter if you have a lot of great AP scores, or just a couple? We examine the data:

# of 5's on AP Exams	Accepted	Deferred/Waitlisted	Rejected	Total	% Accepted
1	392	192	177	761	51.51116951
2	184	74	76	334	55.08982036
3	152	89	88	329	46.2006079
4 - 5	210	101	83	394	53.29949239
6+	129	50	24	203	63.54679803
Total	1070	494	391	1955	54.7314578

It appears that having six or more scores of "5" on AP exams seems to be have an admission boost, but that may be because the GPA and and strength of schedule itself is strong. The rest of the table shows that the number of 5's doesn't seem to change much. This confirms the wisdom that as long as your counselor is checking off the "most challenging course load" box, you should be fine regardless of how many AP classes you take or what scores you receive.

Academic Index

We've talked a bit about the Academic Index before, but let's recap. It's a number that goes up to 240. It was originally used for athletic recruiting, but every applicant gets an AI to serve as a snapshot of their academic performance. The higher your AI, the stronger you are academically. The AI is computed by scaling your SAT/ACT, SAT2 scores, and your class rank/percentile. Here is the formula:

SAT = ((Reading score + Writing score)/2 + Math score)/20
SAT2 = (Highest SAT2 + 2nd Highest SAT2)/20
Rank = Based on a scale, either using GPA or percentile.

We computed AI's based on SAT, SAT2, and Rank for the applicant pool and here were the results:

Academic Index	Accepted	Deferred/Waitlisted	Rejected	Total	% Accepted
230+	376	198	161	735	51.15646259
220-229	234	129	125	488	47.95081967
210-219	88	53	46	187	47.05882353
200-209	24	14	11	49	48.97959184
< 200	8	3	2	13	61.53846154

So the admit rate is essentially the same no matter what your Academic Index was. We can ignore < 200 and 200-209 (to a degree) since the numbers aren't as big there, but the top three ranges have hundreds of candidates. Having a high AI doesn't really produce any significant change an admission rates. This confirms what we saw in the individual factor sections—each score/grade is important, but don't worry needlessly about points here and there. Once you're academically qualified, the number is not going to make a difference.

To wrap with a quote from the New York times article on Academic Index:

"More and more people are going to look at those numbers as having more meaning than they should," said Michael Goldberger, the Brown University athletic director who also spent 10 years as the university's admissions director. "I don't think any admissions officer is going to look at an application and say, 'This person has a 223 AI and we need more people in that category.'"

Go for high scores but remember this is just a threshold to cross. You're not benefitting from retesting for sky-high scores once you already have pretty great ones.

Extracurricular/Supplemental Factors

This section is all about your activities and supplemental factors (teacher recommendations, counselor recommendation, interview, etc). Everything is non-academic. The stuff here isn't as quantitative as the academic factors, but should still prove interesting and useful.

Extracurriculars

The Common Application asks for candidates to write about their extracurricular activities. For each activity, you label how long you've done it, how many hours per week and weeks per year, and you can also discuss your role and any accolades you have received. This will consist of school clubs for most of you, and obviously things like state/national/international awards are impressive.

Naturally, it is difficult to process extracurricular data. This is where humans are incredibly useful and admissions officers are expert, and where computers are not so helpful. How does a machine compare 4 years of varsity crew with 3 years of teaching ballet in the inner-city? We took a two-fold approach: categorized the amount of time spent in each activity, and recorded how many leadership roles (presidencies, captainships, etc) the candidate had. We figured that we can compare "x amount of time in y role" across different activities—not perfectly, but it's better than nothing. Here's what we found:

Admission Outcome	Average Number of Extracurriculars	Average Time (years) per Extracurricular	Number of Students
Admitted	2.08	2.86	220
Deferred/Waitlisted	2.22	2.96	119
Rejected	2.48	3.21	124

So at a high level, the number of extracurriculars reported increased as the admission outcome worsened, but the average time per extracurricular also increased. Common wisdom says that you want to be a "T" profile—good at a couple of things but distinctive in one thing. Time can be a proxy for distinctiveness, but it's hard to conclude anything. Especially because the sample is small, it's unclear if we can take away anything big. One thing's for sure: most of the candidates in this high-end pool had 2-3 extracurriculars and spent about 3 years on each activity. They don't have many activities of 1-2 years, but rather consolidate on a few.

We now delve into the specific breakdown of years per extracurricular:

Year(s) in an extracurricular	Number of Activities if Accepted	Number of Activities if Deferred/Waitlisted	Number of Activities if Rejected
1	1.12	1.36	1.05
2	1.38	1.39	1.46
3	1.31	1.32	1.54
4+	1.62	1.61	1.6

The first column refers to how much time is spent in an activity. So if a poster said "marching band 3 years," we would record it in the 3 row. The "Number of Activities if [x]" indicates how many activities of this type the poster reported i.e. if you wrote "4 years marching band, 4 years tennis," then your number of activities in the 4+ row would be "2".

The intent of this is to show how many activities people reported of each year span. It appears that 4-year activities are the most common, followed by 2 and 3-year activities. Nothing seems to cause an admission difference; having 4-year activities didn't automatically make you better.

Another interesting metric is the quality of the extracurricular. What did you actually do?

Admission Outcome	Average Number of Extracurriculars	Average Number of Leadership Positions	Number of Students
Admitted	2.08	2.18	220
Deferred/Waitlisted	2.22	2.25	119
Rejected	2.48	2.43	124

The takeaway? Looks like everyone has leadership positions. Just listing positions like "Captain" or "Co-chair" doesn't seem to get you much in isolation. The quality of what you do actually matters.

Essays

Now we're getting into the really subjective parts of the application. With extracurriculars, at least you can quantify the amount of time spent. You can't just say, "oh I spent 20 hours on my essay so it's a 7/10," haha. Instead, we used a text sentiment analysis library (TextBlob) to analyze the polarity and subjectivity of student descriptions about their essays. The idea is to see if a student's confidence in their essay positively correlates with admissions outcomes.

Just to give you an idea of how the program works, here are some samples:

```
>>> s = TextBlob("I'm the greatest")
>>> s.sentiment
Sentiment(polarity=1.0, subjectivity=1.0)

>>> s = TextBlob("neutral")
>>> s.sentiment
Sentiment(polarity=0.0, subjectivity=0.0)

>>> s = TextBlob("grass is green")
>>> s.sentiment
Sentiment(polarity=-0.2, subjectivity=0.3)

>>> s = TextBlob("I'm the worst")
>>> s.sentiment
Sentiment(polarity=-1.0, subjectivity=1.0)

>>> s = TextBlob("I tried to make them humorous and revealing of myself as a person (and concise).")
>>> s.sentiment
Sentiment(polarity=0.3, subjectivity=0.8)
```

Polarity ranges from -1.0 to 1.0, and subjectivity ranges from 0.0-1.0. Polarity refers to whether the text is about something good or bad, and subjectivity is about how biased the text is. So the real purpose of this analysis is to see how well you can evaluate your own essays. Here's the data:

Admission Outcome	Average Essay Polarity	Average Essay Subjectivity	Number of Students
Admitted	0.28	0.54	1645
Deferred/Waitlisted	0.3	0.58	936

Rejected	0.3	0.57	725

So basically there's no difference between essay polarity/subjectivity and admission outcome. That suggests that students aren't good at gauging how good or bad their essays are. We can dig into this a bit more by only looking at essay polarities above and below a threshold, i.e. you were really happy or unhappy. The results:

Essay Polarity Threshold	Accepted	Deferred/Waitlisted	Rejected	Total	% Accepted
polarity < 0	177	102	112	391	45.27
polarity > 0	1273	754	548	2575	49.44
polarity > 0.3	715	440	360	1515	47.20
polarity > 0.5	343	220	180	743	46.16
polarity > 0.7	122	64	56	242	50.41

And that's the nail in the coffin. No matter how positive or negative you were, the admit rates were basically the same. **You are not good at evaluating your own essay.** In the last section of the book we'll talk about specific tips for essays and a totally different approach for how to evaluate your essays.

Teacher Recommendations

The Common Application has an entire section for teacher recommendations. There's the demographic info about the teacher, and then these questions on the teacher's background with the student:

- How long have you known this student and in what context?
- What are the first words that come to your mind to describe this student?
- In which grade level(s) was the student enrolled when you taught him/her? (9,10,11,12,Other)
- List the courses in which you have taught this student, including the level of course difficulty (AP, IB, accelerated, honors, elective; 100-level, 200-level; etc.).

Nothing too crazy. The next section is about ratings. There are sixteen categories:
- Academic achievement
- Intellectual promise
- Quality of writing
- Creative, original thought
- Productive class discussion
- Respect accorded by faculty
- Disciplined work habits
- Maturity
- Motivation
- Leadership
- Integrity
- Reaction to setbacks
- Concern for others
- Self-confidence
- Initiative, independence
- OVERALL

and the teacher can choose one of eight ratings for each category:
- No basis
- Below average
- Average
- Good (Above average)
- Very good (well above average)
- Excellent (top 10%)
- Outstanding (top 5%)
- One of the top few I've encountered (top 1%)

Please note that these ratings are relative to the other students in your class year, so your teacher is *literally ranking you against your peers.*

The last part is a written evaluation. Most students don't actually see these ratings, so it's hard to evaluate what your teacher wrote. However, many students comment on their relationships with their teachers as a proxy for how good the recommendations were. And how accurate are students at gauging the impact of their recs? Let's find out:

Admission Outcome	Teacher Rec Polarity	Teacher Rec Subjectivity	Number of Students
Admitted	0.44	0.55	1315
Deferred/Waitlisted	0.43	0.55	662
Rejected	0.48	0.58	530

These numbers are all about the same, which parallels the essay story. At a high level, no clear difference in polarity or subjectivity; everyone thought they had good teacher recommendations. It is interesting that students had much more positive thoughts on teacher recs than on their own essays, probably because they are judging the relationship and not the actual words written.

Let's segment it by different levels of polarity:

Teacher Rec Polarity Threshold	Accepted	Deferred/Waitlisted	Rejected	Total	% Accepted
polarity < 0	36	29	23	88	40.91
polarity = 0	213	108	68	389	54.76
polarity > 0	1066	525	439	2030	52.51
polarity > 0.3	829	410	368	1607	51.59
polarity > 0.5	527	274	256	1057	49.86
polarity > 0.7	285	139	111	535	53.27

This is somewhat interesting. If the polarity is positive, i.e. more enthusiasm, then you can't really differentiate between the admission outcome. So if you were positive on your teacher recs, you can't really say how positive you are. But if you were negative about the recommendations, or simply not enthusiastic, then the acceptance rate was correspondingly lower—**there's a 10% drop in acceptance rate if you're negative about teacher recs**. I would argue that it's tricky to use that "polarity < 0" row because it's only 88 people, but the lesson seems to be that **you can't judge your teacher recs, but if you don't feel great about the teachers, then pick new ones!**

Counselor Recommendation

We briefly delved into the Counselor Recommendation by discussing the Common App Secondary School Report (CASSR) in the Course Load section. It is good to study that section to understand what is asked. Beyond the counselor's demographic information, and the school questionnaire (how many AP/IB courses, describe the GPA scale), there is a whole section for the counselor to comment on you. There are two initial questions:

- How long have you known this student and in what context?
- What are the first words that come to your mind to describe this student?

The counselor has limited screen space to answer these and they're supposed to be more "high level" and overview-y. After that there's a ratings section, with four categories:

- Academic achievement
- Extracurricular accomplishment
- Personal qualities and character
- Overall Rating

and the counselor can check one of eight options for each category:
- No basis
- Below average
- Average
- Good (Above average)
- Very good (well above average)
- Excellent (top 10%)
- Outstanding (top 5%)
- One of the top few I've encountered (top 1%)

These are the same as the options from the teacher evaluation. The final part is the evaluation, which basically asks the counselor to describe you and why they assigned these ratings and just provide more context about you. They can also elaborate on whatever they'd like the adcoms to focus on.

The story here is similar to the teacher recs—you can't really know what's written or how your relationship is conveyed on paper. The data says:

Admission Outcome	Counselor Rec Polarity	Counselor Rec Subjectivity	Number of Students
Admitted	0.35	0.47	1900
Deferred/Waitlisted	0.32	0.46	1089

Rejected	0.29	0.44	901

Counselor Rec Polarity Threshold	Accepted	Deferred/Waitlisted	Rejected	Total	% Accepted
polarity < 0	111	83	67	261	42.53
polarity = 0	557	321	284	1162	47.93
polarity > 0	1232	685	550	2467	49.94
polarity > 0.3	956	511	380	1847	51.76
polarity > 0.5	669	350	259	1278	52.35
polarity > 0.7	301	153	109	563	53.46

Very similar story to the teacher recommendations. **There's a 10% drop in admit rate if you were negative about your counselor rec.** On average students are less optimistic about counselor recs than they are about teacher recs. This is probably skewed due to large schools which have less counselor interaction, so you're just "one of the good kids" instead of clearly the top student who the counselor knows well.

In terms of polarity, being negative had a notably lower acceptance rate than being positive, but if you were positive then it didn't really matter how positive. The implication is the same as teacher recs, except you generally can't pick your counselor. Start building this relationship early and you can avoid being negative and avoid the drop. Counselor recs definitely matter, and you're not a good judge of how good they are, but you can tell if it'll be not good.

Interview

This is also a very interesting question: how much does the interview matter for college admissions?

Can we quantify that impact? Like most of the supplemental factors section, this is difficult to do because students are pretty bad at judging how well the interview went. The data speaks for itself:

Admission Outcome	Interview Polarity	Interview Subjectivity	Number of Students
Admitted	0.21	0.38	1738
Deferred/Waitlisted	0.21	0.42	965
Rejected	0.18	0.32	795

Interview Polarity Threshold	Accepted	Deferred/Waitlisted	Rejected	Total	% Accepted
polarity < 0	143	98	56	297	48.142
polarity = 0	652	307	386	1345	48.48
polarity > 0	943	560	353	1856	50.81
polarity > 0.3	576	315	223	1114	51.71
polarity > 0.5	304	153	128	585	51.97
polarity > 0.7	144	61	63	268	53.73

This data suggests two things: students were generally less happy about how their interviews went, and that admission rates were consistent no matter how they thought the interview went.

We know from anecdotal evidence that interviews are important, but as more of a final piece and not something heavily weighed. The data seems to reflect that, since acceptance rates are so consistent across the polarities. Interviews can sometimes bring insight into a candidate, but they usually just confirm what's in the rest of the application and serve as a check rather than a new piece of info.

Demographic Factors

This section is about your environment and background. We'll look at some things like income, location, gender, and ethnicity and see how they impact the admissions process.

Financial Aid

Most top schools are need-blind, which means they ignore financial need when making an admissions decision. Some schools have Early Decision programs which may take into account ability to pay, but that's not relevant for the cohort that we examined (Ivy League + Stanford + MIT). Looking at the stats, it checks out:

Requested Financial Aid?	Accepted	Deferred/Waitlisted	Rejected	Total	% Accepted
Yes	278	204	148	630	44.13
No	115	67	56	238	48.32

The small % difference can be attributed to variance in sample size (238 "No's" vs. 638 "Yes's"). All these schools are need blind and the data confirms that.

The reason that the "No's" may have a higher acceptance rate is because if they didn't request aid their family income must be quite high, which implies more resources to develop themselves and put together a better application, which would result in a better admit rate. In either case, requesting financial aid doesn't make a difference by itself, but you already knew that ;)

High School

Does it matter if you go to public school or private school? Simon says:

High School Type	Accepted	Deferred/Waitlisted	Rejected	Total	% Accepted
Public	1296	762	626	2684	48.29
Private	351	183	154	688	51.02

NO! Here, Private is grouped as private schools, prep/boarding schools, and parochial schools. We may have missed some school types, but the samples are massive as is. There's no bias for public or private schools; it's all about what you do once you're there. This supports everything that we saw in the Counselor Report section—you are evaluated in the context of your environment and not against an absolute standard.

Ethnicity

This is a very sensitive topic. We know that college employ affirmative action, and underrepresented minorities (URM) have an advantage in admissions. It's not our interest to talk about what kind of admissions boost you get because that's too difficult to quantify, and it doesn't change much—you have no control over your ethnicity. Nonetheless, here's the raw data:

Ethnicity	Accepted	Deferred/Waitlisted	Rejected	Total	% Accepted
Asian	639	410	394	1443	44.28
Black	94	20	23	137	68.61
Hispanic	141	53	43	237	59.49
White	761	515	407	1683	45.22

Note: There is some bucketing done, i.e. "Chinese", "Japanese", "Indian", etc. are categorized as "Asian". [Asian/Black/Hispanic/White] are the ways people most commonly describe ethnicity on the forums so that's what we used.

Whites and Asians were the largest groups and they have nearly identical acceptance rates. Blacks and Hispanics have much higher admission rates, but the sample sizes are also much, much smaller. Even so, using a Z-test calculation for two population proportions, the results are statistically significant at the 0.05 and 0.01 thresholds.

Please note the biased sample here though. College Confidential posters tend to be very competitive candidates, as evidenced by the overall high acceptance rates, so simply being a minority won't help you out unless you're also a competitive applicant. The stats suggest that being a competitive applicant who is *also* a minority does get you a solid boost. Let's add average SAT scores into this computation:

Ethnicity	Average Accepted SAT	Average Deferred/Waitlisted SAT	Average Rejected SAT	Number of Students
Asian	2297	2288	2265	1443
Black	2162	2165	2148	137
Hispanic	2165	2165	2163	237
White	2236	2262	2243	1683

Same story here: all the differences are statistically significant. The samples aren't random so we can't draw conclusions on the population as a whole, but if you're an applicant with competitive scores (which would be the College Confidential population), then you have a better chance of getting in if you're a minority. Nothing earth shattering here, and remember that admissions is holistic, so we can never make guarantees since extracurriculars, recommendations, and many other things also play a role.

We wanted to do more granular analysis i.e. fixing the number of extracurriculars and recommendation sentiment to compare people who are "equal on paper," but the samples were too small to make any real conclusions off of.

Gender

This one is just for fun. I think we all could've guessed that being male or female doesn't affect admission rates. Some posters identify as genders other than Male/Female but we omitted them from our grouping for simplicity. The stats:

Gender	Accepted	Deferred/Waitlisted	Rejected	Total	% Accepted
Female	842	452	327	1621	51.94
Male	1026	651	608	2285	44.90

This is actually surprising. I would've expected similar acceptance rates, but the massive samples and statistical techniques indicate that the differences are significant at any significant level (0.05 or 0.01).

Another issue might be overrepresentation of a school in the sample. For example, it's known that the MIT admission rate is twice as high for females as it is for males. Let's redo our male/female analysis excluding all MIT candidates:

Gender	Accepted	Deferred/Waitlisted	Rejected	Total	% Accepted
Female	708	384	285	1377	51.42
Male	885	458	481	1824	48.52

All of a sudden the difference is not statistically significant at $p = 0.05$ or 0.01, so statistically the populations are equivalent. It's a little difficult to apply standard admission measures since we have a biased sample (College Confidential posters), but I think it's safe to say that males and females have basically the same admit rates at top schools. Even at a place like MIT, the admission rate may be higher but you still have to meet the high admission standards so it's not easier to get in despite what the stats suggest.

Family Income

One would expect wealthier people to have greater access to resources and thus have an easier time getting in, but the stats suggest the opposite:

Income	Accepted	Deferred/Waitlisted	Rejected	Total	% Accepted
0 - 50k	229	124	111	464	49.35
50 - 100k	355	206	183	744	47.72
100 - 150k	92	88	61	241	38.17
150k+	136	107	79	322	42.24

As income increases, the acceptance rate drops. I think this is because of the sample here: high achieving students who are mostly similar grade/extracurricular wise. If you achieve that while coming from a low-income background or a poor neighborhood, it stands out more than if you did it in Bethesda, Maryland.

Factors We Ignored

There are a couple factors that are provided by College Confidential posters that we ignored. Here's a quick rundown of what they are and why we ignored them:

- **Job/Work experience** - many students didn't have this, and it was too difficult to categorize.
- **Volunteer/Community Service** - Some students provided hours of time, others provided years, and it's difficult to compare between those two.
- **Summer Activities** - Hard to quantify this. For example, attending a Brown Summer Session would be distinctive if you're low-income and that's your first exposure to that kind of thing, but not very special if you've done summer programs every summer.
- **Major Awards** - Too much repetition here. Many kids were National Merit Semi Finalists and had some form of AP award. Some kids had medals at the International Olympiads, and that is hugely distinctive and not relevant for the average applicant.
- **Major** - This varies too much from school to school, and students change majors frequently at top institutions. Schools have stated they don't really consider your declared major. To detect a strong science or engineering or humanities bias, the essays, coursework, and extracurriculars are all more relevant.
- **State/Country** - I'm just being lazy here. But the data isn't that useful—you can Google any school to see where their admits come from, and the answer is that it's all over the United States and a handful in various other countries.
- **Hooks** - Students write their own hooks here. The issue is that it's hard to categorize, and most students don't understand what hooks are. A terrific teacher recommendation is not going to be your hook, especially when you can't evaluate what's terrific and what's not.
- **Strengths/Weaknesses/Why** - This section is where the student lists what they thought their strengths/weaknesses were and why they think they got in. I don't think it adds much beyond the other data we're collecting. It's also difficult to analyze since sentiment isn't useful here.
- **Other Results** - This section is about where else you were admitted/rejected/waitlisted. It will be interesting to see the school map for a certain type of applicant, but I'm not sure the data is actionable. I'd like to do this in the future.

As always, the data is available on our website so please take a look there if you want access to the raw source.

Conclusion

So to recap what we've learned through the data analysis:

ACADEMICS

- **SAT:** Aim for a 2200+.
- **ACT:** Aim for a 33+.
- **GPA:** Higher is always better. There's a notable drops in admit rate after your GPA goes below 3.8.
- **Rank**: Higher is better. Being in the top few percentiles is about the same, so don't stress about being #1/#2.
- **Course load:** Be in the 'most demanding' category—this is school specific.
- **AP scores:** Aim for 5's, but students with 3's/4's had about the same admit rate. Absolute number of 5's doesn't seem to be a big difference.
- **Academic Index:** Not a differentiator by itself. 220+ is sufficient.

So for academics, thresholds are the main issue. For your test scores, if you're above the thresholds, then admission rates don't dramatically change. That indicates that it's the other stuff in your application that makes or breaks you. College officers have told us this for a long time and we've always been skeptical, but the data backs it up. To be an "academic superstar," you'll need big time awards. Simply having strong test scores and grades won't cut it.

EXTRACURRICULARS

- Don't do multiple 1-2 year activities. It's better to do a few 3-4 year activities.
- However, students tend to have more 4+ year activities than not, so don't just go for time. You have to think about what you can get out of them and how that's conveyed in your application.
- Having leadership positions wasn't significant.
- You are bad at evaluating essays and interviews.
- If you aren't excited about teacher/counselor recs, there is a big drop. You can't tell how good they are if they're positive, but you can tell when they're negative.

DEMOGRAPHIC

- Doesn't matter if you apply for financial aid.
- Doesn't matter if you're high school is public or private. All about what you do with the resources there.
- **Ethnicity:** If you have competitive scores, you have a better chance of getting in as an underrepresented minority (URM). But that's known as a "hook."
- **Male/Female:** Admit rate is about the same. The female admit rate is higher than the male rate at MIT, but the applicant pool is competitive enough that the standards are the same.
- **Income:** If you're strong academically and average otherwise, it's better to be low-income than not. Being low-income can present a more interesting "story", and being

very high income probably gets you special opportunities, but being mid-high income i.e. 100k-150k has the lowest admit rates in our sample.

Behind The New Strategy For College Admissions

What Is This Section About?

First off, take a deep breath. Whew. We've just gone through a ton of analysis and numbers, and I'm sure your head is spinning. Mine definitely is. So before reading this chapter, just walk around, take a break, and don't come back until you feel mentally alert.

This is the best part of the book. Based on all the data, we're going to describe the optimal strategy for college admissions. This assumes you're the typical kid in a typical high school, preferably in 9th or 10th grade but 11th grade works too. If it's your senior year then it's too late to enact most of the strategy, but you may benefit from the test scores part.

This strategy also assumes that you don't go to a top boarding school or high school and don't have any national or world-class accomplishments. If you did, you wouldn't need the guide.

And with that, let's get started.

Table Stakes

The Table Stakes section refers to fairly standard "metrics" that you need to hit. If you look back at the data analysis and the admissions process, it breaks down into two fairly basic parts:

1. Make sure the applicant is academically qualified
2. Figure out how they'll contribute to the school. Gauge their potential.

Your grades, scores, and to an extent extracurriculars will contribute to #1. Your essays, recommendations, and extracurriculars will contribute to #2 and help build your "image". This involves condensing your whole profile into a few paragraphs.

This section is short because it focuses on #1. If you're not academically qualified, you are not going to get into a top school. While the definition of "academically qualified" varies, the data analysis helped us find thresholds above which the admit rate doesn't change much. Here's the quick summary:

- **SAT:** Aim for a 2200+.
- **ACT:** Aim for a 33+.
- **GPA:** Higher is always better. There's a notable drops in admit rate after your GPA goes below 3.8.
- **Rank**: Higher is better. Being in the top few percentiles is about the same, so don't stress about being #1/#2.
- **Course load:** Be in the 'most demanding' category—this is school specific.

That's literally it. You can be admitted without hitting these metrics, but if you do hit them, you can be confident that you've satisfied criteria #1 and won't be rejected due to academics. At the same time, if you're hitting these metrics, then trying to do more in this section is not going to be an effective use of your time.

And that's it for table stakes. Once you hit this, the other parts of your application are much more interesting. And what's what we'll discuss in the next few sections.

Writing Your Story

Ok, so you've hit your table stakes—the metrics that make you solid academically and put you in a position for further consideration. That takes care of point #1, which is the academic criteria. Now we have to look at #2: "figure out how you will contribute to the school. Gauge your potential."

The admissions officer and other reviewers will try to understand who you are and what makes you tick. They'll look at what activities you do and how you'll contribute to campus. There's a common myth that schools are looking for certain roles, i.e. a saxophone player for an orchestra or something like that. It's all nonsense—every school has multiple acting/musical/singing/skill groups and there's no spreadsheet with skills that need to be found. There is definitely an intent to sculpt a class, but it's at a much higher leve,l i.e. sports, activities, good mix of majors, not at the granular level of specific activities or interests.

You may also hear that some schools are looking for more engineering or more humanities students, but you can't just change your activities on the fly and convince anyone that you fit that profile.

So what is one to do? **You have to build an image through your application**. That image must present you as a leader of people and one who is destined to have influence in society. Someone who will contribute to campus life and add a new perspective to the community. A lot of admissions officers are former alums, and they can ask the question "would I hang out with this person on campus?"

The crucial takeaway is that you are **writing a story** about who you are and why you'll be great on campus. Your courses, academics, essays, extracurriculars, and recommendations all have to combine to present a story. That's why it's not just about the number of years in activities or leadership positions, because everyone has those. They all have to tie together so the officer can say "Aha! I get it. You are [x] and that is what makes you unique."

In your application, your extracurriculars and your essays are both things that *you control* in helping you write your story. In the next subsections we'll go into a strategy for each one on how to construct your story.

On Passion

This is going to be controversial. There are many criticisms of the college admissions process, which say that students are turning into robots and are too busy checking off boxes. People say that students should be working on discovering themselves and finding out their "passions". Yet nobody can quite define passion—it is just something that you're supposed to have all the time no matter what.

The reality is that most adults in life don't know what their passions are, and if they did, they sure aren't pursuing their passions. It is silly to expect high school students to somehow magically know what they're passionate about and act on that, especially because people change so much as they grow older.

Furthermore, it's hard for parents to give advice like "just be yourself and follow your dreams!" when most parents are not living their dreams. They didn't follow that advice and struggle to pass on the wisdom to their kids.

There are some precocious youths who are incredible at something and love doing it. They're passionate but they're also disciplined and work hard towards becoming who they want to be. These kids are superstars in the admissions process because there is such a clear body of work that reflects that they are trying to be.

You are not that kid. You haven't figured everything out yet, and you don't know who you want to be, and that's okay. Again, people literally spend *decades* before they know what they really want to do, and even then they don't act on it.

So the first point I want to make is: **don't stress about living your passions**. You have time to figure out what you want to do and who you want to be. It's good to explore, but don't add unnecessary pressure on yourself to "figure it all out" before you turn eighteen.

Extracurricular Strategy

Ok, mini-rant out of the way. The #1 advice most people give to college students is to be passionate about your activities and showcase that through your application. This is technically good advice, but pretty unactionable. That's because most kids follow one of the following strategies:

1. Parents talk to each other, hear about what some kid did to get into an Ivy League school, and ask their child to do the same thing.
2. Kids talk to older classmates, see what strong students in their school are doing, and do the same things.
3. Parents and/or kids go online and see what other kids have done, either from forums or articles, and do the same extracurriculars.
4. Guidance counselor recommends some activities, kids do them.
5. Kids just don't have any extracurriculars, so no strategy.

Do you see the commonalities here? In every case, you are getting advice from someone else and trying to imitate. That makes you similar to other applicants, either current or previous, and thus makes you less memorable to the committee. There's a saying that "all stereotypes have some truth to them," and this is especially true for college admissions. If you're a high scoring Asian student who plays violin and tennis, it'll be very difficult to stand out since so many other people will have a similar background.

That's why our entire extracurricular strategy is based on *standing out*. You want to present a story about yourself that is memorable, and that by nature implies that it's different from the typical stuff. That's why doing a potpourri of extracurricular activities doesn't do you much good—nothing really stands out and so you seem more typical. Lots of kids play sports or do theater; it's fine if you enjoy it, but you can't just base your application around them.

Schools want T-shaped students, i.e. people who are good at a broad array of things but really exceptional at one thing. They want to build a well-rounded class by gathering a collection of really pointy, T-shaped people. If you try to be well rounded, i.e. a jack of all trades, then you're not going to be memorable. Thus, signing up for a bunch of clubs is not going to do you any good for college admission results because it's not different from anything before.

So how do you actually stand out? If you're young i.e. in 8th, 9th, or 10th grade, explore a lot of clubs and activities and immediately filter out stuff that you don't like. Find one or two things that you can really get behind, and stick with them throughout high school. You want the longevity in 1-2 activities so you can show a long-term commitment to something, which is a positive trait in itself.

Beyond that though, it's not enough to just be a four-year athlete or act in dramas for four years. That's because a lot of people do the same thing.

This is where the bulk of our extracurricular strategy comes in. You've got one or two keystone activities, but how do you translate that into a story about yourself? Easy, you combine it with other interests. Let's say you're a strong math student and you also play basketball. Then you can start blogging about basketball analytics and reach out to others in the industry and try to publish your analysis. You can start a basketball camp and use math/physics to encourage students to learn hard things and apply them in real life via sports. You can even combine your two extracurriculars, i.e. if you like swimming and theater, then start writing screenplays about dolphins and swimming in the ocean or whatever you want.

It's hard to be great at the world or national level at any one activity. If you can do that, absolutely go for it. But if not, the next best thing is to be in the top 20% in two things and tie them together. Most students who apply tend to be in the top 50% of their activities, so they don't stand out at all. But if you can tie your activities together and tie that to your intellectual interests, then you have not only unique experiences but also a bunch of things that tie together and help unify your story.

Finally, I just want to reiterate that you want to avoid things that are stereotypical or things that other kids are doing. If you do what everyone else does, you'll get what they get, which is generally a rejection. Having unique activities helps, but it's also important to combine activities and interests to build up your story and express more typical activities in unique ways.

It's like chess; you want to use your pieces in combination to attack!

Essay Strategy

Ok, so we've got the extracurriculars, and we're combining our interests to express them in different ways. We're focusing on one or two key activities and doing unique things that will stand out, or at the very least not be the typical stuff like National Honor Societies, standard school clubs, minor awards but nothing great, etc.

You already have a leg up with the extracurricular strategy, but you can fully leverage that via the essays. First off, here are a few books on writing the college essay:

- *50 Successful Harvard Application Essays: What Worked for Them Can Help You Get into the College of Your Choice* by Staff of the Harvard Crimson
- *On Writing the College Application Essay, 25th Anniversary Edition: The Key to Acceptance at the College of Your Choice* by Harry Bauld
- *50 Successful Ivy League Application Essays Paperback* by Gen Tanabe (Author), Kelly Tanabe (Author)

You don't have to get all of them or any of them, but there are two things you must do:
1. Read a ton of admitted student essays. Try to figure out what they do well and what they don't do well.
2. Read up on clichéd college essay topics and **avoid them at all costs**.

The second point is particularly important. It's hard to write a great college essay, but it's easy to avoid writing a bad essay. The biggest thing is to not write about clichéd topics. This includes things like:

- Volunteering somewhere and then just talking about what you did.
- Overcoming an injury or some hardship
- Talking about role models
- Talking about one moment where you thought you'd fail but you "found courage and persevered" and everything turned out great.
- Talking about how you traveled to/from somewhere and found out that people are all the same.

There are many, many examples of the above, and we can't go into the details, but just Google around and you'll find so many examples of clichéd topics. People love writing these essays because they are completely oblivious to this fact:

You are not a special snowflake. Most of the things you've done have been expressed before.

College essay advice often talks about your "voice" i.e. showcasing who you are. Unfortunately, this turns into talking about *what you've done*, which they already know from your essay. In addition, the lessons you learned are mostly exaggerated because you can't say something like "I traveled to Tibet and realized how important it is to disconnect from technology and be in tune with nature" and expect anyone to form an impression of you. Anyone could write something like that—what is it about *you* that makes that statement true or special?

To provide a contract, imagine if you wrote "I wanted to be in tune with nature, so I stopped using technology for a year". Now that's crazy. You can make the same sentiment, but the story is so much more unique because it's about you. Giving up technology for a year is something that people can imagine but would find hard to believe, so the essay naturally piques our curiosity. You can then proceed to write about what you did and how you felt, and that's how your voice really comes out.

However, that's not enough. Just because you can express your voice doesn't mean you're expressing something relevant. Remember how we talked about writing your story? Well, your essay has to not only reflect something about you, but also reflect something that complements what you've listed in the rest of your application. So if you're a math loving basketball player who does theater, then your essay could be about how you tied these activities together to write a play about the physics of basketball. Your extracurricular combinations are different from most people's so your essay's core topic becomes more interesting, and after reading advice on cliché busting and expressing your voice, you'll know how to convey what you did and how you felt to round out your story.

One final piece of advice, and this is probably the most useful thing:

Have someone who doesn't know you read your essay and then write a paragraph about what they think of the author.

This is the number one thing that a college essay writer can do to get feedback. Unfortunately, most people get feedback from their parents, teachers, and friends, who all know the writer well. You need to find strangers who have no context so they can give you an objective opinion about how you come off based on the essay. Most kids think they're highlighting their achievements and showcasing worldly knowledge, when they might actually be full of hot air. If there's anything we learned from the self-evaluated data, it's that people are bad at evaluating their essays and recommendations. Get honest, blind feedback, and revise your essay until it reflects what you want it to. This is a tiring process, but rewriting is the heart of rewriting, so start your essays months in advance and keep revising.

The essay is one thing that's completely in your control and can make or break your application, so put in the time and get the feedback and make things happen.

What To Focus On For Recommendations

So the previous section covered writing your story and what *you* can do to write that story. One other integral part of the application is the teacher and counselor recommendations. You don't control this, but often times teachers and counselors don't know how to write appropriate recommendations. Too many times they focus on "what you did" or generic accolades instead of backing them up by example. So what you should do is find teachers who've taught you in a few classes, preferably AP/IB/Honors classes, who like you, and link them to this MIT blog post on recommendations. This is by far the best advice I've found on writing recommendations. These are the points they recommend you address:

- What is the context of your relationship with the applicant? If you do not know the applicant well and are only able to write a brief summary, please acknowledge this.
- Has the student demonstrated a willingness to take intellectual risks and go beyond the normal classroom experience?
- Does the applicant have any unusual competence, talent or leadership abilities?
- What motivates this person? What excites him/her?
- How does the applicant interact with teachers? With peers? Describe his/her personality and social skills.
- What will you remember most about this person?
- If you have knowledge of MIT, what leads you to believe MIT is a good match for this person? How might he/she fit into the MIT community and grow from the MIT experience?
- Has the applicant ever experienced disappointment or failure? If so, how did he/she react?
- Are there any unusual family or community circumstances of which we should be aware?

Your teachers need to focus on describing who you are to support their comments, and they need to highlight things that aren't in the rest of the application. The recommendation is usually a great place to talk about your character and non-academic personality, so help your teachers understand what's expected and how they can help you out.

Expectation Setting

This is a good time to take another breather. There's lots of advice in this chapter and it'll be good for you to take a break, and then reread parts of the chapter to make sure you understand and can act on the advice given.

There is one last point I want to make, and that's on expectations. You can do everything "right" and not get into your dream school. That's because there are thousands of talented kids who are trying to do the same thing and there are no guarantees. Imagine the admission process like shooting arrows at a target. By studying hard and having engaging hobbies, you can build a compelling profile—that's like getting better at archery. The top schools are all on the target board, and maybe you have a top choice, which is the bull's eye, but there are no guarantees. This book will improve your archery skill and make you more likely to *hit the target*, but you're not guaranteed anything.

Let me be clear: there is **nothing** you can do to guarantee admission. Some people can donate millions or make some influential phone calls, but if you fall in that category, you're not going to be reading this book. There are people who are less qualified than you who will be admitted, as well as people who are more qualified. You should never be bitter about the outcome—just be proud that you gave it your best shot and live with the results. Life is what you make of it, and getting into or not getting into a specific college is not going to change that.

Conclusion

If you're not like me, you jumped straight here. Not cool to jump to the end of the book—the other sections are pretty great! If you are like me, then you've read and skimmed your way here and can reap the fruits of your efforts.

In this section, we wrap up everything and summarize the game plan.

What We Learned

Given the student population we looked at, having high test scores and a solid mix of extracurriculars and recommendations/essays is enough to get about a 50% admit rate at top schools. The data can be broken down into the following key points (reproduced from a previous section):

ACADEMICS

- **SAT:** Aim for a 2200+.
- **ACT:** Aim for a 33+.
- **GPA:** Higher is always better. There's a notable drops in admit rate after your GPA goes below 3.8.
- **Rank**: Higher is better. Being in the top few percentiles is about the same, so don't stress about being #1/#2.
- **Course load:** Be in the 'most demanding' category—this is school specific.
- **AP scores:** Aim for 5's, but students with 3's/4's had about the same admit rate. Absolute number of 5's doesn't seem to be a big difference.
- **Academic Index:** Not a differentiator by itself. 220+ is sufficient.

So for academics, thresholds are the main issue. For your test scores, if you're above the thresholds, then admission rates don't dramatically change. That indicates that it's the other stuff in your application that makes or breaks you. College officers have told us this for a long time and we've always been skeptical, but the data backs it up. To be an "academic superstar," you'll need big time awards. Simply having strong test scores and grades won't cut it.

EXTRACURRICULARS

- Don't do multiple 1-2 year activities. It's better to do a few 3-4 year activities.
- However, students tend to have more 4+ year activities than not, so don't just go for time. You have to think about what you can get out of them and how that's conveyed in your application.
- Having leadership positions wasn't significant.
- You are bad at evaluating essays and interviews.
- If you aren't excited about teacher/counselor recs, there is a big drop. You can't tell how good they are if they're positive, but you can tell when they're negative.

DEMOGRAPHIC

- Doesn't matter if you apply for financial aid.
- Doesn't matter if you're high school is public or private. All about what you do with the resources there.
- **Ethnicity:** If you have competitive scores, you have a better chance of getting in as an underrepresented minority (URM). But that's known as a "hook."

- **Male/Female:** Admit rate is about the same. The female admit rate is higher than the male rate at MIT, but the applicant pool is competitive enough that the standards are the same.
- **Income:** If you're strong academically and average otherwise, it's better to be low-income than not. Being low-income can present a more interesting "story", and being very high income probably gets you special opportunities, but being mid-high income i.e. 100k-150k has the lowest admit rates in our sample.

What To Do With That Knowledge

Given this, you should work to hit your academic thresholds, but don't worry about anything beyond that. You don't need to be a testing machine. Have one or two activities that are unique for your environment, do them for several years, and build around them in your essays and recommendations.

Don't worry about summer camps or service trips or things that you "heard" are good to do. At the same time, don't waste your summers either. You should be looking to do something that is really unique and in line with your application. Remember that unique for your environment is not the same as unique for the application pool. For example, if you like science and do research at a university, that might be very special for your school, but many other kids are doing stuff like that. The best strategy should use two or more of your interests and combine them in ways that others haven't. So if you like science but you also like flying kites, then maybe you start a group to help people build and battle kites and the starter kits help students learn math and physics to make the best kites.

There are a lot of ways to stand out, but you have to try. It's not about racking up years or activities or positions; what is going to make you memorable?

The demographic stuff is outside your control. That's life. Do your best and move on. Again, the stuff in this book is not going to guarantee admission anywhere, but it will help you understand what's possible and presents one strategy for admissions. At the end of the day, you have to create the best profile for yourself and leave the rest up to luck.

If I had to summarize it all in one sentence: "Have sufficiently high academics, and be expert and/or unique at something."

Is It Worth It?

Like I said in the beginning, I went to a fun and interesting high school, but it was middle-tier academically. I spent a lot of time reading about how to go to a top school, worked hard and did some cool stuff. I ended up with a pretty competitive profile and got into several great schools and decided to attend Yale.

I had a great four years there. I studied Computer Science, rowed for the Lightweight Crew team, participated in hackathons and intramural sports, and tons of other things. I learned a lot and made great friends who I'm proud to call friends for life. I can go on and on, but the point is that I was really happy then and am proud to be a Yale alum.

I think you can have a great college experience at hundreds of schools, because it's largely about you as a person. What are you doing to make the most of your time there? But to the rest of the world, your alma mater becomes a powerful signal that you are smart, capable, and worthy of attention. I've just graduated and work at Google, so I can't comment on years of advantages due to my background. However, so far I have had so many positive interactions just because I'm a Yale alum. I remember being a senior in high school and reading a comment that said "Congrats on your admission! Yale is lucky to have you, and you should enjoy the time before college, because once you attend, the Yale name will be with you forever and all your interactions will reflect that." I didn't grasp the gravity of the statement, but it's very true. I'll now always be seen as not just Aayush, but as Aayush the Yale grad.

So I think you benefit a ton from going to a top school, and that sticks with you throughout life. It's a big advantage and something that you don't fully realize until you get much older. I think in the digital age the importance of college will diminish, but it's still a huge deal.

So is it worth it? Absolutely. I think you should put in the time to have great grades and scores and activities, and challenge yourself to do interesting things. But this is what I would recommend to someone even if they weren't trying to get into a top school. It really boils down into goals versus systems. You can have a goal to get into an elite college and do what it takes for a few years, then coast through school, get some cushy jobs, and live a pedestrian life. But if you develop a system where you try to maximize the utilization your time and maximize your learning, then you'll find that you get so much more done every day and that aggregates to massive achievements over a lifetime.

I don't want to ramble on too long, but I hope you get it. I wrote this book to distill all the things I've learned to save a lot of other kids the hundreds of hours it'd take to learn all this. I hope you can use this information to get into your dream school, or a top school, but even if you don't, have solace in the fact that you learned a lot along the way and did interesting things. People like that are the ones that everyone remembers in life.

Best of luck.

Appendix

This section attempts to build an applicant profile by school. We present stats on the following fields:
- Unweighted GPA
- SAT
- ACT
- Rank
- Number of Extracurriculars
- Number of Leadership Positions
- (Average) Years in an Extracurricular
- Academic Index

For each field, we present the average and median stat, as well as the number of students that reported this i.e. the sample size from which we computed average/median.

Some of the entries don't have many results. In general, if there are fewer than 100 students reporting, then you should take it with a grain of salt. In addition, we don't filter by admission result (Accepted/Deferred/Rejected) because the goal is to show what an applicant looks like. Since this data is from College Confidential, naturally this represents the higher end of applicants in terms of scores and activities, so keep that in mind.

Finally, you'll see that the "Number of Leadership Positions" stat has way more entries than "Number of Extracurriculars" or "Years in an Extracurricular". That's because for the former we just look for things like "President", "Captain", "VP", etc, while for the latter two categories we are looking for time spent in an extracurricular. Lots of people report their position but not how long they did the activity, so the leadership stat has more entries than the years stat. The total number of extracurriculars stat uses the smaller value, so the number of students is always the same for "Number of Extracurriculars" and "Years in an Extracurricular", but always less than the "Number of Leadership Positions" stat.

Have fun!

Brown Applicant Profiles

Brown	Average	Median	Number of Students
Unweighted GPA	3.9	3.95	250
SAT	2221	2250	275
ACT	32.8	33	153
Rank	5.18	2	189
Number of Extracurriculars	2.4	2	58
Number of Leadership Positions	2.01	2	229
Years in an Extracurricular	2.97	3	58
Academic Index	224.86	226.66	139

Columbia Applicant Profiles

Columbia	Average	Median	Number of Students
Unweighted GPA	3.9	3.95	132
SAT	2251	2270	135
ACT	32.83	33	71
Rank	3.87	2	91
Number of Extracurriculars	2.18	1	22
Number of Leadership Positions	2.27	2	104
Years in an Extracurricular	2.92	3.23	22
Academic Index	228.55	230.83	68

Cornell Applicant Profiles

Cornell	Average	Median	Number of Students
Unweighted GPA	3.89	3.95	172
SAT	2187.36	2220	182
ACT	32.46	33	96
Rank	6.04	3	132
Number of Extracurriculars	1.82	1	38
Number of Leadership Positions	2.14	2	135
Years in an Extracurricular	2.82	2.8	38
Academic Index	223.64	224.17	91

Dartmouth Applicant Profiles

Dartmouth	Average	Median	Number of Students
Unweighted GPA	3.93	3.98	91
SAT	2263	2290	107
ACT	33.48	34	54
Rank	4.34	1	74
Number of Extracurriculars	2.52	1	21
Number of Leadership Positions	2.32	2	91
Years in an Extracurricular	3.16	3.2	21
Academic Index	228.33	232.08	54

Harvard Applicant Profiles

Harvard	Average	Median	Number of Students
Unweighted GPA	3.94	4	374
SAT	2261	2300	398
ACT	33.8	34	141
Rank	2.8	1	267
Number of Extracurriculars	2.1	1	59
Number of Leadership Positions	2.46	2	293
Years in an Extracurricular	2.84	3	59
Academic Index	229.27	231.5	197

MIT Applicant Profiles

MIT	Average	Median	Number of Students
Unweighted GPA	3.92	3.98	404
SAT	2256	2290	349
ACT	33.98	34	127
Rank	3.66	2	266
Number of Extracurriculars	2.86	1	7
Number of Leadership Positions	2.76	3	17
Years in an Extracurricular	2.77	2.6	7
Academic Index	228.24	230.33	107

Note that the extracurricular data for MIT is too small. We included it here just for completeness.

Penn Applicant Profiles

Penn	Average	Median	Number of Students
Unweighted GPA	3.91	3.96	232
SAT	2243	2260	277
ACT	33.14	34	135
Rank	4.18	2	212
Number of Extracurriculars	2.11	1	55
Number of Leadership Positions	2.26	2	196
Years in an Extracurricular	2.99	3	55
Academic Index	226.27	228	153

Princeton Applicant Profiles

Princeton	Average	Median	Number of Students
Unweighted GPA	3.95	3.99	268
SAT	2282	2300	280
ACT	33.38	34	103
Rank	3.7	1	218
Number of Extracurriculars	2.19	1	43
Number of Leadership Positions	2.16	2	201
Years in an Extracurricular	2.98	3	43
Academic Index	229.1	230.67	159

Stanford Applicant Profiles

Stanford	Average	Median	Number of Students
Unweighted GPA	3.94	3.98	490
SAT	2253	2280	478
ACT	33.6	34	223
Rank	3.9	1	358
Number of Extracurriculars	2.36	2	70
Number of Leadership Positions	2.29	2	262
Years in an Extracurricular	3.08	3	70
Academic Index	227.87	230.17	256

Yale Applicant Profiles

Yale	Average	Median	Number of Students
Unweighted GPA	3.94	4	452
SAT	2267	2295	448
ACT	33.8	34	216
Rank	3.13	1	353
Number of Extracurriculars	2.19	1	93
Number of Leadership Positions	2.44	2	379
Years in an Extracurricular	3.06	3.25	93
Academic Index	229.42	230.83	255

29132899R00050